for Jan —

Enjoy!

Walking is for yourself and for what you can be or become. You are exercising for yourself in your own way. You are doing what you do, as well as you can, because you enjoy it.

walk—

don't run

a natural approach to

- exercising
- eating
- living

by elvira monroe

Wide World, Inc.
P.O. Box 476
San Carlos, CA 94070

Library of Congress Catalog Card Number: 79-63351
ISBN: 0-933174-04-7

Printed in the United States of America.

to Mia, Steve and Kate
May we always walk in love

TABLE OF CONTENTS

Introduction
REDISCOVER YOUR LEGS

Few things are good for everyone. Fewer natural.

Yet, walking is perhaps the one activity unique to us—natural to us—taken so for granted—which is best for us.

It is undoubtedly because it is *so* natural to us, that we have passed over it to don jogging outfits or pound tennis and racquet balls.

Aware of the need to exercise, we've embraced one sport after another. Most of us have forgotten how to walk.

It is not my intent to put down these sports. I continue to endorse running, even as I have in the book I co-authored, *Run For Your Life*. It is the exploitation, which I deplore. The activity turned fad.

Many people have asked me whether the exercise *had* to be running. If there wasn't another way to get exercise as beneficially? They've confided that they had trouble sustaining a running program.

Guiltily they speculated, "What's wrong with me? I don't like to run."

Others resented the Madison Avenueing of running, and did not like being associated with something so "in."

Weather posed a problem for some, and a place to run a problem for even more.

As I looked around me, and as I listened, I too began to ask if it *had* to be running.

Realizing that through my book, I'd been part of the "running is for everyone" pitch, I felt an obligation to ask questions.

I too had been taken aback by how apologetic non-runners were, and by the complacent air of superiority of some runners.

And so in considering alternatives I came to the obvious—walking.

---

*To recapture the walking experience in America through the centuries, I recommend *Walking in America,* ed. by Donald Zochert, Alfred A. Knopf, New York, 1974.

"Slow Down—You Move too Fast—Got to Make the Morning last"

—Simon and Garfunkel

SLOW DOWN

The pace of our lives is frantic. We race everywhere, pushing to meet schedules. Consider the loaded phrases with which our language abounds: "I ran into him downtown." "I'm just going to run (or dash) to the store." "He is running around with her." "She is always running him down." "She's running for office." *As we run here or there, pressure builds—and with pressure, stress.* And so the double meaning of this book's title.

Start walking through life. You will be in better shape physically, psychologically and emotionally. Life will be less stress-filled, and more fun.

When on vacation or traveling in other countries, one senses a different pace. At first we may be impatient at the difference. If we relax and adapt to the new tempo, we discover that we feel less tense. Taking a deep breath, we assess the change in how we feel. We recall those studies on lower blood pressure and fewer heart attacks. But this is vacation, we rationalize.

Naturally our pace is slower. But can we sustain this vacation pace, once we return home? Yes! By reassessing priorities. By making time, and asking how you want to feel? Are you moving so fast, life is a blur? *If so, slow down to a walk, and live more fully.*

Eye Nature's walks, shoot folly as it flies,
And catch the manners living as they rise;
Laugh where we must,
be candid where we can,
But vindicate the ways of God to man.

—Essay on Man
Alexander Pope

THE AIR WE BREATHE

Awareness of our polluted environment and of our fuel shortage, should act as an additional impetus to get us walking, and keep us walking.

Helping in this way, is also helping our health, and that of others.

Consider how we angle for the spot closest to the grocery or department store, often circling again and again to get a few feet nearer. Or, how we move our cars to avoid walking that extra block.

Every time we drive needlessly, we are contributing to the problem. *We must get up out of our car seats and be counted as caring.*

Change is the hallmark of today's and tomorrow's world. Sudden, continuing, rapid change.

In order to guide change, rather than be controlled by it, we must be aware. We must be especially aware of change while it takes place.

The work for change always starts with ourselves. It is carried on by many different people in many different places, but it is the same work.

The crises of environment demand of us a commitment to change *our* ways.

Look at the branch, a bird, a child, a rose, or anything God ever made that grows.

—Edwin Arlington Robinson
Sonnet

WHERE TO WALK

Walk around the block. Walk to the store. Walk to visit a friend. To the library. To church. To a movie.

When tempted to drive anywhere, always consider walking.

It makes sense to start your walking program around where you live. You are familiar with the area, and can better judge how far you want to go.

Look around you. Observe houses for sale. The mailman's route. Greet neighbors, children playing. A friendly "hello", not a conversation. It is important to keep going. Socialize another time.

If you are sensitive to the rhythm and changes in your neighborhood, it will never be the same.

Even so, we all want change. A new walkway is the best way to keep you walking.

Seek out new places, even if it means driving to them. So you drove there. So what! Don't feel guilty or apologize. Just get out of the car and walk.

Acquire a street map. Use it, mark it up. Duplicate portions of it. No need to cart around a paper accordion.

As you develop a collection of places to walk, you might want to share and exchange the information with fellow walkers and friends. Don't forget to rate walking areas, making note of good and bad features.

Some areas are walkable in all kinds of weather. Others are seasonal. Explore and discover for yourself the blossoms, the best sunrise, the brisk breeze.

If you live or work in the city, walking can be faster than a taxi, and certainly much less frustrating than waiting for the bus.

Walk your total being. As you walk, you will grow more and more in tune with yourself.

—our own chained feet,
Walk freely as the waves that beat
Our coast.

—New England
James Gates Percival

OTHER PLACES TO WALK

There are good books outlining hikes and walks in your area. Do investigate them.

Hiking in the foothills, for example, is walking. But, it does require planning and arranging to fit it into your daily schedule. It is not an everyday activity. Walking can be.

Yet, hiking is not to be overlooked.

My preference is walking along the beach. But not everyone is fortunate enough to live so close to the beach.

Look for *your* special area near you. From this area a new interest may grow from a pebble, a dried weed, a landscape.

If there is public transportation in your area, board a bus or mini bus and ride to the end of the line or to a stop which interests you. Get off, and start your explore-a-walk.

The important thing is to maintain an ongoing walking program. Make walking part of your daily routine, if possible.

If you are content to walk the same area, that is your choice. I know a couple in their seventies, who, when they cannot take their usual neighborhood walk, use their patio to exercise. Walking back and forth, they almost seem to be pacing. To them it is the sustained exercise that is important. The opinion of others incidental, irrelevant.

There are a number of groups which emphasize walking or hiking as part of their programs. You might want to check your local Sierra Club chapter to learn of its offerings. Added to the other benefits of walking, is the social one of meeting new people as you participate in a nature walk.

Girl Scouts and Campfire Girls, Boy Scouts, the Y and other youth groups all have outdoor programs in which you might want to become involved. They provide yet another way to reach out and to help educate young people about walking.

"What do you suppose will satisfy the soul, except to walk free and own no superior."

—Laws for Creations
Walt Whitman

WHEN TO WALK AND HOW OFTEN

Try to walk every day. If you establish a routine for yourself, you will be more likely to sustain your walking program.

Perhaps a walk before or after work is best for you. Perhaps a walk at lunch time. *Your* time to walk is as individualized as your schedule.

The important thing to remember is that walking takes time, and you must learn to *make* time for it. We miss so much by rushing around. Walking can be the brake that slows us down to a pace of awareness and appreciation.

How often have you driven by people walking, and wondered why they were on foot? Was something wrong with their car? Had they missed the bus? Had their doctor recommended exercise? Wasn't it your last consideration that they might be walking by choice?

Even though you have taken your "daily walk", it does not

mean that you shouldn't continue to walk during the day and evening whenever possible. Learn to integrate walking into your daily life. Choose walking, rather than driving. It will not be easy, nor will it always be possible. But try to make your choice walking whenever you can.

Health is the vital principle of bliss,
And exercise, of health.

—The Castle of Indolence
James Thomson

MOTIVATION

KEEP WALKING

What better motivation than walking because it is good for you and makes you feel better?

Even as many of us walk to stay healthy, others are walking to help regain or improve their health. More and more doctors are recommending walking after heart attacks or other cardio vascular problems.

Walking is healthy, enjoyable and enriching. Make it, and keep it, a part of your life.

Because it may help keep you walking, you may want to consider a log book of where, when and how far you've walked. Listing may serve as that extra motivation you need. Even the most dedicated walkers experience the temptation to put off, so don't feel guilty. Walking can be fun, but because we have been away from it so long, we must reeducate ourselves.

We must resist the prevailing attitudes of society, and discipline our minds and bodies.

Perhaps, rather than a log, a journal is for you. A journal in which you would record reactions, feelings, not necessarily day by day, but as an expression of yourself.

Maybe you'll want to make a notation in your calendar or engagement book. Maybe yours is none of these. The important thing is to keep walking.

Talk about walking. Extol it. The more people you inform of your efforts, the easier it will be for you to keep walking. Each convert to walking will repeat the pattern.

To travel on foot, is to travel like Plato and Pythagoras.

—John Davis

WHAT TO WEAR

The attire for no other sport is so individualized, or economical. The only thing you need to start walking is a comfortable pair of shoes which give support. For women, the shoe should be flat or with a moderate heel. The sturdy oxford, the hiking boot, the running shoe. It's up to you. Old. New. Gardening shoe. Stylish footwear. Whatever. Comfort and support are the main criteria. Other than that, the choice is up to the walker.

Dress to suit the weather. Avoid overdressing. Clothes you shed, only have to be carried.

Comfortable socks, to absorb perspiration, are recommended.

When walking, try to avoid carrying things in your arms or hands, for it will put off your stride. If you are a gatherer and cannot resist picking up seed pods for a dried arrangement, use the pockets in your jacket or coat. Better yet, explore a daypack. It will hold that loaf of bread from the store, those library books, the sweater you've brought along should it turn chilly. Of course, there are times when you cannot avoid carrying something. A briefcase, carried as you walk to the bus or train, comes to mind. A tote bag. Be aware of the effect on your stride. Alternate the sides on which you carry, to avoid strain on the neck and back muscles.

The whole thing about walking is that it is a natural activity, and can be an integral part of our day. If we were more a walking society, a walker would be unnoticed.

But, if we were a society of walkers, I wouldn't be writing this book.

Moderation is best, and to avoid all extremes.

—*Plutarch's* Lives

YOUR STRIDE AND TEMPO

PACE YOURSELF

Brisk. Energetic. Quick. All these describe a desirable walking pace. We are not talking about strolling, but walking as an exercise. Walking at a brisk pace, swinging your arms, uses most of your body muscles, and increases cardio vascular activity.

As you walk, you will eventually take longer steps. Do not push, but gradually lengthen your stride. Your leg muscles will tell you when you are really reaching. Don't overdo, or you may blister or be sore. Pace yourself, and you'll soon be excited by the shortened time it takes you to travel a given distance. You will develop a rhythmic stride.

Should your feet be tired after a walk, try soaking them in epsom salts, dissolved in warm water. After soaking your feet for a few minutes, dip them in cold water. Your feet will tingle!

Some people like to measure how fast and how far. I like to avoid walking by the measuring stick, but for those of you who want to measure, consider four miles per hour as an *ultimate* goal. This averages out to somewhere between 120 to 125 steps per minute.

If, as you walk, especially if you are over fifty, you notice sharp pains in your legs, check with a doctor. Your body could be trying to tell you something. A Disease such as *arterio-sclerosis* sometimes manifests itself with these kinds of pains.

Every life is many days, day after day. We walk through ourselves, meeting robbers, ghosts, giants, old men, young men, wives, widows, brothers-in-love. But always meeting ourselves.

—James Joyce
Ulysses

WITH WHOM TO WALK

Walking can be solitary, or a shared experience. Its focus can be increased cardiac efficiency and lowered blood pressure, or just fun.

Regardless of your emphasis, as you walk you will feel good about yourself. Your muscle tone will improve and your vitality will increase. You won't discover the meaning of life by walking, but you will learn a lot about yourself.

Let the "with whom" shift and change with the patterns of your life. The important thing is to walk.

I listen to the wind
to the wind of my soul.

—Cat Stevens

WALKING ALONE

Lyrics and poems abound with images of the solitary figure walking his or her soul. Undoubtedly walking can be therapeutic. There are many, many times when we cherish or need solitude and time to "think things out." How natural it is to walk at these times. There are times when we wish to get away—to walk symbolically away from what troubles us. In anger or frustration, we can pound a racquetball, work in the garden, clean out closets and drawers. But if we are seeking a communion with ourselves, we need a different pace. A walking one. Walking, we can explore our thoughts, allowing our minds to wonder, freed from the pressures of work, home, school. It can provide a time to sift and sort—to try to work things out—to reexamine ourselves and our goals—to reach within, to all the good that is there.

Society, in making us fearful of solitude, has made us fearful of ourselves. *Walking can help us find a way back to ourselves.*

The great hills of the South Country
They stand along the sea;
And it's there walking in the high woods
That I could wish to be,
And the men that were boys when I was a boy
Walking along with me.

—The South Country
Hillaire Belloc

WALKING WITH ANOTHER

Because of its flexibility, walking need not be solitary. It can be a beautiful time of togetherness, in which you grow closer to one another. Sharing ideas on a regular basis builds trust. As you open up more and more to one another, friendship grows and deepens. You will find that although you may start with superficial conversations, jokes, or gossip, in time you will shift.

This time away from TV and the phone is precious. It is time you've chosen to set aside to be together, to communicate, to perhaps recultivate the lost art of conversation.

You will draw from your surroundings and reach out. The rows of houses, the trees will be part of it. The changing skies. The people. The air. Having left the womb of your home, your world has opened. Even so, have you. And, as you move in this world, you are opening yourself to others. Having learned to trust one person, makes it easier to trust another and another. Trusting is caring, and caring is loving and living. They are all part of the circle of being.

We know what we are, but know not what we may be.

—Hamlet IV 5, 1. 43

WALKING WITH YOUR SON OR DAUGHTER

Our lives are so scheduled, so pressured. And so are our children's lives. We squeeze time together between things we think should have priority. Not making time to be together, we end up feeling guilty.

Invite your son or daughter to walk with you. It need not be all the time. It probably can't be or shouldn't be. Respect their schedules and other interests, but let them know you want them. Be prepared for rejection at first, but do not turn away. Ask again. Don't beg or make them feel guilty. The important thing is to let them know you want them to join you. Any time spent together, helps enhance your relationship. As you walk, it is a wonderful time to listen and share. Please—not a time to give advice, unless it is sought.

You will be doing something together. You will be sharing each other. As you do this, you will grow closer. It may surprise you to find that in time your son or daughter will pridefully tell others of your walks. It is vital, however, that *you* be the one who adapts at the beginning. *Match your strides and you will walk together.*

The four-legged brain of a walk-ecstatic dog.

—Harold Monro

WALKING YOUR DOG

We put out a cat, and walk a dog. Turn that walk into something you enjoy, rather than resent. Something you want to do, rather than have to do. You and your dog will both be happier.

If there are leash laws in your community, train your dog accordingly or your stride will be ludicrous as your dog walks you.

Lack of respect for others has caused legislation in some areas, requiring dog owners to clean up after their dogs. Even without fines and penalties, one would hope that dog owners would train their dogs. This is something you must work out according to the area in which you live.

....gardens with their broad green walks, where soft the footstep falls.

—Mary, Queen of Scots
Henry Glassford Bell

WALKING AND THE YOUNGER CHILD

Most children are active by nature, and are generally involved in some form of athletic activity, organized or otherwise.

Exercise, or the lack of it, is usually less a concern with younger children than with adults. Most school districts have supervised activities. They have teachers who are trained to recognize motor development needs and who encourage healthy exercise. It is not my purpose to deal with exercise, but with attitudes of children toward walking.

We make so much of a child's efforts to walk; of his or her first step. We marvel. We encourage. We record it on film and in baby books. Walking. How wonderful! And then? And then, we proceed to rear that child unaware of the joys of walking.

Children develop attitudes toward walking very early. They come to expect, even demand, being transported to their game, meeting, or friend's house. And so mothers spend hours yoyoing back and forth, schlepping their children. And the children? They have been educated to not walk!

Encourage your child to walk to school, rather than rely on public transportation or a ride. He or she will get up with the wakening world, and with all the magic of its sounds and images.

If sidewalks in your town or city are inadequate or unsafe, organize and demand of the local government that they be improved.

Set an example for your children, and you will change attitudes.

I've been running a long time
on this travelling ground
wishing hard to be free
of going round and round.

—Bitterblue
Cat Stevens

WALKING AS A NON-COMPETITIVE SPORT

Even walking *can* be competitive, and as such, is an event in the Olympics.

But the kind of walking about which I am writing is non-competitive, and free of stress. It can be relaxing, conditioning, enriching, social but, not competitive. There will always be those who compulsively claim they've walked X miles in X minutes X days a week, and ask how far, how fast, how often you've walked. Such a person can get so busy emphasizing measuring, that growing within hasn't taken place. In my opinion, he or she risks missing the real meaning of walking. I do not mean to minimize race walking. It can be exciting and fun. But races, by their very nature are competitive. I am writing about walking, not race walking. *Walking is for yourself, and for what you can be, or become.*

Any competition that there may be is with yourself, in tune with yourself. The growth is *your* growth as a healthier and more aware human being. You are doing what you do, as well as you can, because you enjoy it.

There are no records to be broken. No time to be met. There is *no* way to measure. It is you. *You* are exercising for yourself in your own way. No turf is the same. No rules the same.

Achievement is measured by how you feel—by you.

Bad men live that they may eat and drink, whereas good men eat and drink that they may live.

—Socrates

CHANGING HOW AND WHAT WE EAT

Even as we return to the *natural* way to exercise, we need to return to a more *natural* way of eating. I am not talking about eating nuts and berries, but about *not* eating un-natural additives. I am urging cutting back on the *poisoning foods* of "civilization."

Walking increases cardiac and lung capacity. It promotes weight control. It tones body tissues. But, along with the exercise of walking there must be a change in the way you eat.

The less *salt* and *sugar* you add to food, the better off you are. Tune into the natural taste of foods. Steam your vegetables. Eat fruits instead of sweets. Cut back on red meats.

Above all, start reading labels. Look for breads without preservatives. They are there and they range from wheats to French. I recently needed to buy chili seasoning. As I checked, label after label listed salt as the main ingredient, with a few grains of chili as an incidental. These were the products of major companies. Appalled, I persisted until I found the natural product.

We *must* create a demand for pure foods. I am not suggesting that you necessarily convert to so called "health foods". What I am urging is an examination of your eating habits, and a return to eating more naturally.

I am a great eater of beef, and I believe that does harm to my wit.

—William Shakespeare

EAT NATURALLY

The low-calorie natural foods listed below contain important minerals, vitamins and fiber. They contain the natural fats for the oil your body needs.

The cholesterol controversy has been raging for many years and will undoubtedly continue for many more. My advice in this area, as in others, is to be cautious. Use restraint. Loaded with cholesterol, the diet of the average American taxes the heart. Modify your diet to cut down on saturated (animal) fats. Rely on the goodness of nature's foods and boycott those french fries, doughnuts and potato chips. Cut down on eggs. Consider periodic blood tests for cholesterol levels. Control plus exercise should be your commitment.

Remember—Changing your diet can change your life!

What is food to one may be fierce poison to other.

—Lucretius

NATURAL FOODS FOR SNACKING ENERGY

Natural foods are good for snacking and general well-being. When you want to reach for a cup of coffee or "junk food" try some of the following. You'll feel better, look better, run better.

vegetables	fruits		nuts & seeds
carrots	oranges	prunes	almonds
celery	lemons	mangos	sesame
cucumber	apples	peaches	walnuts
beets	bananas	melons	sunflower seeds
cabbage	papaya	grapefruit	brazil nuts
spinach	pineapple	figs	pumpkin seeds
lettuce	cherries	raisins	cashews
avocados	blackberries	pears	soybeans
tomatoes	raspberries		peanuts
peas	strawberries		pecans
squash	apricots		filberts
watercress	grapes		hazelnuts
			chestnuts

miscellaneous

wheat germ
yogurt
soups
low-fat/not-fat milk
honey
ginseng
lemonade

breads

natural grain breads
gluten bread

Get your sugar this way, too. In fruits. Your body likes it better, absorbs it more slowly.

Naturally, you need to eat—just remember to eat naturally!

A man's own observation, what he finds good of and what he finds hurt of, is the best physic to preserve health.

—Francis Bacon

GUIDELINES FOR FOOD SELECTION AND PREPARATION

- Steam vegetables. A steamer costs under $5.00 and fits into a variety of saucepan sizes.
- Tune into the natural flavor of foods.
- Cut back or eliminate salt as a seasoning in cooking or eating.
- Explore unsalted butter.
- Drink lots of water.
- Use garlic and onion powders, not salts.
- Learn to use herbs as seasoning.
- Cut back on red meat as much as you can.
- Try seasoning fish, meat and chicken with lemon juice.

My appetite comes to me while eating.

—Montaigne

ENERGY DRINKS

Energy-packed, nutritious drinks will make you feel and look healthier.

Indulge yourself, free of the poisoning guilt that used to follow your consumption of sundaes and rich shakes.

Reward yourself with these taste treats and feel good about them and yourself.

Try energy drinks at breakfast, after running, or for a nutritious taste treat during the day.

With a blender you can create new drinks endlessly. Fantasize the day's creation while you are walking.

Don't worry about weight gain. Your body knows how to use natural foods. Craves them.

Above all, don't be afraid to experiment with new combinations.

Only be wary about going overboard with protein. Too much of anything can sometimes be just as harmful as too little.

If you do not own a blender, seriously consider purchasing one. Its availability will make you less likely to put off preparing your energy drinks. Vigorous whipping with a hand beater also works very well.

The amino acids found in protein are imperative for good nutrition.

These are but a few recipes to get you started. As you can see, the drinks can be as varied as your imagination.

Consider adding wheat germ, brewer's yeast, extra honey or bran for extra zest.

The protein (either liquid or in granules) and the lecithin listed in the following recipes are available at health food stores.

No. 1

1 banana
2 cups of skimmed milk, or non-fat milk
1 T honey
2 T protein
1 T lecithin
Put ingredients in blender. Blend 25 seconds. Add 3 or 4 ice cubes.
Whip until frothy.

No.2

1 banana
½ cup pineapple (canned, crushed, or chunks, or better yet, fresh)
1 or 2 T coconut milk (canned, bottled or powdered)
1 cup yogurt
1 T lecithin
2 T protein
Put ingredients in blender. Blend 25 seconds. Add 3 or 4 ice cubes.
Whip until frothy.

No. 3

½ cup pineapple (canned, crushed, or chunks, or better yet, fresh)
1 or 2 T coconut milk (canned, bottled or powdered)
1 cup yogurt or skimmed milk or non-fat milk
1 T lecithin
2 T protein
Put ingredients in blender. Blend 25 seconds. Add 3 or 4 ice cubes.
Whip until frothy.

No. 4

1 banana
½ cup orange juice
2 T honey
1 cup yogurt or skimmed milk or non-fat milk
1 T lecithin
2 T protein
Put ingredients in blender. Blend 25 seconds. Add 3 or 4 ice cubes.
Whip until frothy.

No. 5

1 banana
6 strawberries
1 cup yogurt or skimmed milk or non-fat milk
½ cup orange juice
1 T lecithin
2 T protein
Put ingredients in blender. Blend 25 seconds. Add 3 or 4 ice cubes.
Whip until frothy.

No. 6

1 banana
1 peach
4 apricots
1 cup yogurt or skimmed milk or non-fat milk
1 T lecithin
2 T protein

Put ingredients in blender. Blend 25 seconds. Add 3 or 4 ice cubes.
Whip until frothy.

No. 7

1 cup grapefruit juice
3 T honey
6 to 8 strawberries
1 fresh papaya
1 T lecithin
2 T protein
Put ingredients in blender. Blend 25 seconds. Add 3 or 4 ice cubes.
Whip until frothy.

No. 8

½ cup pineapple
1 sliced apple
1 cup yogurt
1 T lecithin
2 T protein
Put ingredients in blender. Blend 25 seconds. Add 3 or 4 ice cubes.
Whip until frothy.

No. 9

¼ cup sliced apple
1 banana
1 papaya
6 strawberries
1 cup yogurt or low-fat milk or non-fat milk
1 T lecithin
2 T protein
Put ingredients in blender. Blend 25 seconds. Add 3 or 4 ice cubes.
Whip until frothy.

No. 10

½ cantaloupe
6 strawberries
1 banana

½ cup orange juice
1 T lecithin
2 T protein
Put ingredients in blender. Blend 25 seconds. Add 3 or 4 ice cubes.
Whip until frothy.

No. 11

1 cup pineapple juice
¼ cup crushed pineapple
2 carrots, cut up
1 T honey
1 T lecithin
2 T protein
Put ingredients in blender. Blend 25 seconds. Add 3 or 4 ice cubes.
Whip until frothy.

Adequate protein is vital to healthy hair. Without it, hair will be dull and will lack body. It's not enough to rely on protein enriched shampoos. Your diet must include sufficient protein.

LEMON BASE FOR DRINKS

If you are lucky enough to have a lemon tree, or friends who will share their lemons, squeeze the juice and freeze into individual cubes. Store the cubes in plastic bags in your freezer.

They'll be ready for lemonade-mix with honey, not sugar—or as a base,or just to add to your drinks for extra tang.

Have you ever heard of the Sugar-plum Tree?

—Eugene Field

YOUR CHILD'S NUTRITION

Even as we seek to educate our children about exercise, we must educate them about nutrition. Good nutrition means better health. A healthy child is potentially a better adjusted child.

When your child comes home from school, he or she is ravenous. Junk foods give quick satisfaction, but little or no nutrition. Indeed they can slowly poison. Avoid having them in the house. Have instead, a supply of snack foods (See Changing How and What We Eat: Natural Foods).

Children like variety. Provide it. Your investment is in a healthier child growing into a healthier adult. It will be hard to resist the pressures of television, huckstering sugar-coated cereals, cupcakes, snacks. But resist we must.

Children need energy foods. I recommend you give them one of the following energy drinks with breakfast and when they get home from school. Because it is new and different, expect resistance. Dig in, and be positive. Encourage your child to create his or her own concoction. Vary the drink according to the fruits in season and your taste.

Join your child. You will both benefit as you share eating in good health.

The following energy drinks are particularly popular with children:

No. 1

1 banana
2 cups milk
1 T honey
2 T protein
1 T lecithin
Put ingredients in blender. Blend 25 seconds. Add 3 or 4 ice cubes.
Whip until frothy.

No. 2

1 banana
½ cup pineapple (canned, crushed, or chunks, or better yet, fresh)
1 or 2 T coconut milk (canned, bottled or powdered)
1 cup milk
1 T lecithin
2 T protein
Put ingredients in blender. Blend 25 seconds. Add 3 or 4 ice cubes.
Whip until frothy.

No. 3

1 banana
½ cup orange juice
2 T honey
1 cup milk
1 T lecithin
2 T protein
Put ingredients in blender. Blend 25 seconds. Add 3 or 4 ice cubes.
Whip until frothy.

No. 4

1 banana
6 strawberries
1 cup milk
½ cup orange juice
1 T lecithin
2 T protein
Put ingredients in blender. Blend 25 seconds. Add 3 or 4 ice cubes.
Whip until frothy.

No. 5

1 banana
1 peach
4 apricots
1 cup milk
1 T lecithin
2 T protein
Put ingredients in blender. Blend 25 seconds. Add 3 or 4 ice cubes.
Whip until frothy.

When using an energy drink with breakfast, add 1 egg if your child is not already having an egg. This, plus toast or cereal, starts the day in a balanced, healthful way.

Bodily exercise when compulsory, does no harm to the body.

—Plato The Republic

WALKING TO LOSE WEIGHT

Not everyone wishes to lose weight, but those who do, be aware that pounds are not going to melt off as you walk. Weight loss can only be accomplished by curtailing the amount of food you eat, and by a proper diet. Changing your eating habits is the way to change your figure. What an ongoing walking program *can* do, is:

- firm up muscles
- help you lose inches
- slowly lose pounds
- exercise your whole body

You will notice that your clothes will fit differently. Friends will comment on your appearance.

It will happen naturally, because you are exercising your body naturally. You are returning to the oldest method of body conditioning.

Our bodies were exquisitely designed for movement. Rediscover natural exercise.

He gets through too late who goes too fast.

—Publius Syrus
Maxim 767

A DIET TO LOSE WEIGHT

Anyone wishing to lose weight may choose from a smorgasbord assortment of diets. And we do! We leap frog from one diet to another. There is no easy diet. Losing weight requires control and restraint. Forgetful of this, we succumb to the lure of "get thin fast" schemes.

Fast. We want to get rid of the pounds fast. We punish our bodies, and impair our health with these fad diets. Yet, we fool ourselves. Maybe this one. Maybe this time.

Dieters are suckers for gimmicks. A diet must have something different to have appeal. Realizing this, since I too am a member of the club, I share this diet with you. It won't work fast, but it *is* different!

Using it, you have to give up things. We overweight people want to punish ourselves, even as we reward ourselves for overeating.

You won't have to drastically change *what* you eat, only *when* you eat it.

You'll be able to have a glass of wine. Reward.
You won't be able to have coffee. Punishment.
You are eating *people* foods, not dieter's foods. Eating is an integral part of our social life. Food, something we prepare or share in a social way. Accept it as such.

Try this diet. I assure you that you will lose weight steadily. With this diet, coupled with walking, you will lose inches.

When you reach your desired weight, it will be easy to make a transition. You will still need to monitor what you eat, but since you'll be walking, your body will be trim and you'll like the way you look.

I do not present this diet as a panacea. It is only one way to diet. You may have a diet that works better for you. As long as it is nutritionally sound, use it. Moderation is the key word in all weight-loss programs. It was excess that made us fat. Good wishes for success, whatever your program.

Remember not to overdo. No matter how healthful the food may be, it will still add pounds if you don't monitor how much you eat.

THE DIET

BREAKFAST:
Fruit. Period.

MID-MORNING:
Fruit, if you are hungry.

LUNCH:

I. Choose *one:*
bread
rice
lentils
beans (navy or kidney)
potatoes
pasta products

You may use a *small* amount of butter with any of these.

II. One, two or even three vegetables, either raw or cooked preferably steamed)
Bonus: 1 glass of *dry* wine

DO NOT EAT: eggs, cheese, yogurt, milk, meat, fish, chicken, cottage cheese

MID-AFTERNOON:
Fruit, if you are hungry

DINNER:

I. Choose *one:*
Meat (lean)
fish
chicken (without skin)
cottage cheese
yogurt (plain)
eggs (not fried)
cheese

You may use a *small* amount of butter or oil to cook if necessary.

II. Green salad—as much as you want. Try combining different salad greens. Try a spinach salad. Use a light oil and vinegar dressing.

DO NOT EAT: bread, rice, potatoes, beans, lentils, pasta products, or fruit.

MARTYR LIST:

AT NO TIME HAVE:

coffee
tea
carbonated drinks, even if sugar free
hot chocolate
sugar in any form
jams, jellies, honey
candy

A FEW SUGGESTIONS

LUNCH

BEANS WITH CELERY

Soak beans overnight. Drain.

1 cup white navy beans
4 cups water
1 onion (chopped)
8 stalks celery (chopped)
1 clove garlic, minced

Bring to a boil. Lower heat and cook for about two hours over low heat. Drain off all but a small amount of liquid. Serve.

LENTIL SOUP

1 cup lentils
1 onion (chopped)
3-4 carrots (sliced)
4 celery stalks (chopped)
6 peppercorns
1 clove of minced garlic
1 bay leaf
4 cups of water

Bring to a boil. Lower heat and cook two to three hours over low heat. Serve.

POTATOES WITH ONIONS

1 baking potato
2 green onions (minced)
1 tablespoon butter
a dash of pepper

Boil potato until cooked, but not mushy or too soft. Cut into 2″ pieces. Add butter, onions, and peppers. Toss.

RICE WITH CELERY AND ONIONS

1 cup steamed rice

Add celery, onions (chopped very fine)

Season with a dash of soy sauce when served.

2 stalks celery
3 green onions
1 tablespoon oil

In skillet, stir fry celery, onions in oil. When softened, but before browned, add rice. Continue to stir fry for 2 to 3 minutes..

EVENING

A BASIC CHEESE OMELETTE

1 egg
a dash of garlic or onion powder.
1 teaspoon water
2 to 3 tablespoons of shredded cheese (either Monterey, cheddar or Swiss)

Beat with fork or wire wisk until blended. Do not overbeat.

Melt 1 teaspoon of butter in a skillet, making sure butter covers surface of pan. Pour eggs into skillet. Cook until it grabs the bottom of the pan. Angle the pan, so that as you tilt, the uncooked egg seeps under the cooked part.

Pat top of omelette with fork. Reach under making sure it isn't sticking.

Add filling of 2 to 3 tablespoons shredded cheese.

Fold into three parts, covering the filling as you do so.

BASIC SALAD DRESSING/OIL AND VINEGAR

Equal parts oil and vinegar. Adjust according to taste.
Add garlic powder and/or oregano if you want.
Try grinding black pepper over salad after you've tried it.

About the Author

After a varied career in volunteer groups and local politics, Elvira Monroe returned to teaching eight years ago.

A keen awareness of the role eating plays in our lives has led her to the conviction that good eating can mean good health—especially if combined with walking or running. She is co-author of *Run for Your Life* and *San Francisco—A City to Remember* and editor and designer of *Exploring Point Reyes* and *The Mystique of the Wilderness.*

Due for release this spring is *Greek Menus and Moods.*

Walking is the one activity unique to us—natural to us—taken so for granted—which is best for us.

It is never too late to start a walking program. It is only too late to continue putting off starting.

Are you moving so fast, life is a blur? If so, slow down to a walk, and live more fully.

If we were more a walking society, a walker would be unnoticed. But if we were a society of walkers, I wouldn't be writing this book.

Society in making us fearful of solitude, has made us fearful of ourselves. Walking can help us find a way back to ourselves.

Start walking through life. You will be in better shape physically, psychologically, emotionally.